Practical

CONTAINER GARDENING

David Carr

The Crowood Press

First published in 1992 by
The Crowood Press Ltd
Ramsbury, Marlborough
Wiltshire SN8 2HR

This impression 1994

British Library Cataloguing-in-Publication Data

A catalogue record for this book is available from the British
Library

ISBN 1 85223 621 3

Acknowledgements

Artworks by Janet Sparrow
Photographs by Sue Atkinson except for the following: page
15 (bottom) and page 59 (bottom right) kindly supplied by
Sutton Seeds Ltd: pages 14 (bottom left), 20 (top left) and 57
by S Wooster; page 16 (top) by Larchlap; pages 22 (top left),
30 (right) and 48 (bottom) by Dave Pike; pages 23, 32 (top
right), 36 and 46 (bottom) by Bryn Photos.

Thanks to: Mrs M Atkinson; Rex Cheatham, Mrs I Gibbon,
Mrs B Powell, and Mrs A MacWilliams of Bracknell
Horticultural Society; Ms Ellie Grigas; Ms Louise Hill,
Shurlock Row, Berks; Mrs Joan Moss; Mrs Anne Noble; The
Royal Horticultural Society, Wisley, Ripley, Surrey; Mrs L
Rutterford, Dorney Reach, Bucks; Pauline Sheppey, Garden
Cottage Nursery, Farnham, Bucks; Mr Simpson, Kennedy's
Garden Centre, Windsor, Berks; Mr and Mrs Softly, Sidbury,
Devon; Mrs Jean Williams, The Nag's Head, Sunningdale,
Berks; and The Willow Garden Centre, Windsor, Berks.

Typeset by Chippendale Type Ltd, Otley, West Yorkshire
Printed and bound by Paramount Printing Group, Hong Kong

CONTENTS

INTRODUCTION

Container gardening has much to offer, both in its own right and as an added bonus to an existing garden. Introducing plant-filled containers of one sort or another gives great scope for ornamental displays around the home, growing fresh fruit and vegetables can become a reality in what would otherwise be impossible situations, and the foundations of an absorbing hobby are laid.

Consider the finer points. Plants can successfully be container grown in situations where the soil is infertile, polluted or otherwise unsuitable. They can be introduced on to hard surfaced areas or grown at height, as with hanging baskets, window-boxes and wall baskets. Plants which might be 'lost' when planted directly into the garden border will stand a good chance of capturing attention when grown as single specimens.

The best way of creating a focal point with a few plants is to mass them together for effect. Containers are ideal for displaying short-term bedding plants in due season. Finally, plants can be restrained when grown in containers – and their growth rate controlled – by root pruning and varying the size of the container.

There are, however, limitations to container growing, and these should be taken into account at the outset before embarking upon any project. Plants are totally dependent upon the grower. Daily watering is, for instance, vital during the growing season and regular attention to feeding and potting is necessary. Plants are vulnerable to the weather. Their root anchorage and the anchorage of their supports are not as firm as their counterparts planted directly into the garden border, and so they are likely to be damaged by high winds in exposed gardens. Plants also need protection from winter wet and frost.

Successful container growing depends on a suitable choce of plants in the first place. Some plants stand up to root restriction and to the temperature fluctuations typical of container growing better than others. Suitable containers and composts must be used and plants should be sited according to their needs. Subsequently, containerized plants must be given adequate care and attention with particular regard to watering, feeding and taking steps to bring them safely through the winter.

Container plants add colour and soften an otherwise severe setting.

1 • PLANT SELECTION

ntroducing containerized plants into the arden calls for just as much planning as vith any other garden project. Don't rush to uy containers and plants in a haphazard ashion – pause for a while. First decide on ne required overall effect and then on the ating and type of individual containers.)nly when you have done this is it possible) select suitable plants.

iting Containers – Some deas

void positioning containers where they will e exposed to strong, drying winds or will be n permanent shade, and pay particular heed to draughts whistling through between buildings. In very exposed situations, plants and containers can be damaged, and poor flowering, scorched foliage and ailing plants are commonplace.

Focal pointing A single container, stood prominently on a hard-surfaced patio is a popular, simple and effective way to create a focal point. Tree and shrub planters are well suited for the purpose, as are bowls, urns, troughs and sinks. Where space allows, some gardeners prefer to group several containers as a focal point.

Doorways and steps As with focal pointing, simplicity is the key to success. Framing doorways and entrances with pairs of matching containers is a conventional

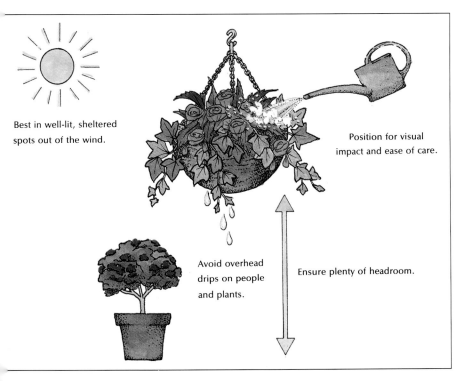

Best in well-lit, sheltered spots out of the wind.

Position for visual impact and ease of care.

Avoid overhead drips on people and plants.

Ensure plenty of headroom.

ause a while before hanging your basket – there are several important points to onsider.

With a little imagination, a group of plant-filled containers will make a striking focal point. Here an evergreen conifer, a herbaceous blue Agapanthus, *and yellow bedding begonias and pansies look well.*

approach. Conifers are a popular choice of plant in this situation, but short-term bedding plants also look good. If the cost of two containers is prohibitive or if they look overpowering, try just one. Arrangements need not be symmetrical to look 'comfortable'. If you have steps in your garden, a pair of matching urns will often provide the finishing touch. Where containers are used near doors and steps, never block the way – a minimum clearance of 3ft (90cm) is needed.

Window dressings Window boxes, and high-level wall and hanging baskets will all add the height which is often lacking in small garden planting schemes.

Wall relief Consider setting wall boxes and hanging baskets at various levels. But be ever mindful of the need for regular watering, and of the need to keep hanging baskets well above normal head-height and positioned where drips are unlikely to be a nuisance. Perhaps free-standing containers of climbing or wall plants would be better.

Matching urns placed on either side of some steps create dimension and add relief.

1 *Kochia* (burning bush)

2 *Impatiens* (busy Lizzie)

3 *Helichrysum petiolatum*

raditionally, doorways are flanked with matching containers. Here bedding plants are used for
ummer display. Red Impatiens *give impact when backed with the pale green foliage of* Kochia
nd edged with grey-foliaged Helichrysum petiolatum.

edding plants and bulbs are hard to beat for a spring display by the front door. Pink tulips and
ellis *could be contrasted with blue forget-me-nots, as here.*

1 pink tulips

2 blue *Myosotis* (forget-me-not)

3 pink *Bellis* (double daisy)

An eye-catching window-box where geraniums and petunias contrast with grey foliage.

Rafter clothing Rafters make good frame-works for climber displays, and subsequently form the foundations for a cool, restful oasis on a hot summer's day.

Waysigning A strategically placed trough or two, or a row of patio containers, will soon pinpoint 'no-go' areas.

Camouflaging Downspouts can be hidden neatly from view with a container-grown climber or wall shrub. A climber-clad trellis will divert attention away from dustbins and other necessities of life, while standing a patio container over a manhole cover will conceal it.

Plant Selection

Plant choice is a largely a matter of personal preference. But for success, allow your preferences to be influenced by the nature of the setting, and resist impulse buying. Instead, set out with a shopping list, having first worked through a simple check-list to

A free-standing trellis panel, fronted with a trough-planted Cotoneaster horizontalis *and* Euonymus fortunei *will make little work and conceal the dustbin nicely.*

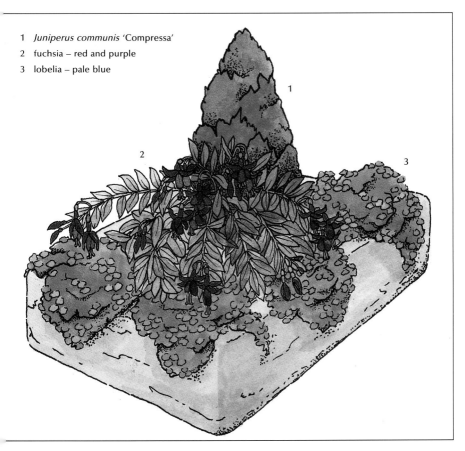

1   *Juniperus communis* 'Compressa'
2   fuchsia – red and purple
3   lobelia – pale blue

A sink-type container is often used to conceal a manhole cover. Here Juniperus communis 'Compressa' is used with a succession of bedding plants in due season – fuchsia and lobelia for summer display.

stablish each plant's suitability for the pur-ose in hand.

Plant needs   It is important to match a plant's needs to the prevailing site condi-ons, taking into account such things as ardiness. A plant's hardiness is its ability to grow, flourish and overwinter outdoors, and so is a critical element for success. Hardiness varies enormously from one plant variety to another. Check locally at your garden centre, bearing in mind that plants in containers are more likely to suc-cumb to winter cold than similar plants grown in beds and borders. Establish which containers are in exposed positions and which are sheltered, and choose plants accordingly. Consider light intensity too, and select plants suited to full sun or partial shade, depending on the position of the container.

Types of plants   There are two main groups of container plants. First are the so-

Camellias make fine container subjects. (Left) A camellia. (Right) A double camellia.

Erica carnea and pansy.

Pelargonium (ivy-leaved geraniums)   These cascading geraniums are excellent summer bedding plants for hanging baskets and patio containers. But all bedding geraniums with their free-flowering habit and colourful blooms are suitable. Use them as accent plants or for massing. A warm, sunny, sheltered position is preferred.

Erica carnea (winter and spring flowering heathers)   Low growing, these heathers are suitable for window-boxes and troughs, and as edgings. Depending on the variety, the evergreen foliage is golden, green or bronzed, and the clusters of bell-shaped blooms can be pink, purple, carmine, red or white. Lime-free compost is preferred.

called bedding plants. Quick maturing and short lived, they occupy their display containers for a maximum of eight months. Spring bedding plants are set out in autumn and flower early in the year, while summer bedding plants are set out in early summer and bloom through to autumn. For brilliance of colour and length of flowering season, few other plants can equal bedding plants. When spring and summer bedding follow in succession, expect flowering to commence in late winter and continue, almost without a break, until autumn.

The other main group of plants is the long-lived and permanent group. These plants occupy their display containers over a certain period of years. During this time they are moved into progressively larger containers.

Permanent plants come in many guises: there are woody stemmed trees, shrubs and conifers, well suited to growing singly as a

(a) Set out tallest plants first, starting them at the centre of containers which are viewed from all sides. (b) Start planting at the rear of front-facing containers.

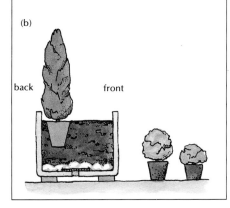

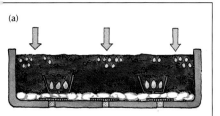

(a) In mixed plantings, as the first stage, set out bulbs either loose or plunge-planted. (b) Then interplant with other bedding between the bulbs.

feature; there are herbaceous border plants for patio displays; and there are also diminutive dwarf rock or alpine plants, used extensively in sinks and troughs. Some of these permanent plants are evergreen while others drop their foliage or die back in autumn. For year-round foliage interest, evergreens are invaluable, with conifers ranking with the best.

Bonus plants It is worth seeking out plants with double-bonus qualities. This

Petunia An attractive, compact, very floriferous, adaptable summer bedding plant, unequalled when massed in containers of most types. Their brilliant, dazzling flowers come in many colours. Resisto mixed F1 hybrids, are particularly good, being dwarf plants bred for weather tolerance. They are at their best in sunny, sheltered positions.

Houttuynia cordata 'Chamaeleon' A creeping herbaceous border plant with vivid aromatic variegated leaves in reds, yellows, bronzes and greens. Use on their own or with other plants in patio planters and window-boxes. Shelter from midday summer sun and drying winds, and give frost protection in cold areas. Must not dry out.

These geraniums and clivia make an imposing window-box display – seen in France. The contrast in colour is most striking.

may be flowers plus attractive foliage, fruit or scent as an added feature.

Size and shape of plants What is the best size and shape of plant to suit the setting and the container? Pay heed to the ultimate size of plants, not the size at planting. Permanent plants with quick growth rate are likely to outgrow their welcome.

Colour Simple colour schemes of, say, two colours or colour shadings are the most likely to succeed. Contrasting one colour with another gives maximum impact – as with red and gold. Colour shadings of the same colour make restful harmonies – try pink with red or cerise.

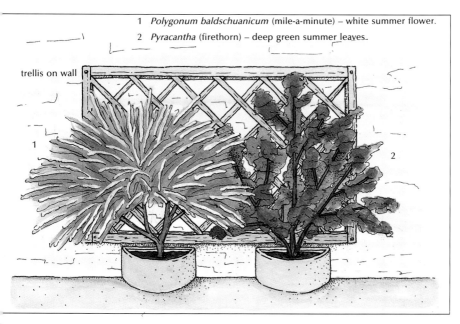

1 *Polygonum baldschuanicum* (mile-a-minute) – white summer flower.
2 *Pyracantha* (firethorn) – deep green summer leaves.

trellis on wall

1

2

Polygonium baldschuanicum (mile-a-minute) will smother out most of its neighbours during summer, and is too invasive for confined spaces, unless it is trimmed regularly.

Pansy mixed with lobelia.

Viola (pansies and violas) Cheerful and stunningly coloured in rich, clear, bright shades of yellow, red, orange, blue, purple, mauve and white. Traditionally, these weather-tolerant, neat dwarf plants are used for edgings in mixed containers of spring bedding. But some varieties make good summer bedding, too, when given partial shade.

Buying Plants

Aim to buy from a garden centre or nursery so that a visual assessment can be made. Be wary of prepacked plants from overheated supermarkets, as when such plants are planted outdoors they often suffer a severe set-back. Read the label, paying particular attention to the variety. This is the last name and is usually given in 'inverted commas' – *Campanula* 'Stella', for example. *Chamaecyparis lawsoniana* illustrates the importance of variety – the varieties of this species vary from about 20in (50cm) to 20ft (6m) in height!

Trees and shrubs Opt for container-grown plants. They establish quickly and can be moved at most times of the year, provided the weather is suitable, although roses are an exception as the majority are still sold with their roots exposed. Select plants

Aucuba japonica 'Variegata' (spotted laurel)   A most tolerant evergreen specimen shrub which reaches about 5ft (1.5m) in height. Grown for its large, glossy, leathery, green-splashed-yellow leaves which show up best in the sun. Will carry scarlet berries if a male variety is planted nearby.

Conifers of different heights, placed in a row or grouped together, provide year-round interest. Ornamental shapes created by clipping are an extra feature.

which have a good overall shape with well-spaced branches. Avoid evergreens which have gone bare at the base — new foliage rarely breaks away again. Plants should be firmly anchored in their containers and you should avoid any which are drying out, with the compost shrinking away from the sides of the container, and any where the surface is weedy and covered with moss. Steer clear of plants which you find standing in draughty passageways. Avoid those which have grown too big for their pots and with excessive top growth and exposed

Begonia semperflorens   Showy summer bedding plants. Small, waxen, brilliantly coloured flowers are produced in profusion throughout summer on 6–9in (15–23cm) high plants. The plants are started off in the spring. In the autumn they are lifted from their beds and are discarded.

Impatiens (busy Lizzie)   Invaluable continuous, free-flowering, small, bushy, compact summer bedding plants. Noted for their brilliance and clarity of colours in many hues. Blooms are massed to smother the foliage. Use as edgers or main plantings in all manner of containers.

Betula Golden Cloud' (golden birch)   This graceful deciduous shrubby tree reaches 10ft (3m) in height and is best grown as a specimen. The golden spring leaves take on rich summer hues and the colour is held until leaf fall. Shelter from cold or drying winds is needed, as is protection from hot midday sun.

Tagetes (French marigolds)   A reliable showy summer bedding plant suited to most container types. Use for both mass planting and edging – be guided by plant height. These bushy plants flower freely and continuously through summer and autumn in yellows, oranges, mahogany-red and bronze. There is great variety of flower form.

)ots – when repotted they will be reluctant) grow away, especially if they have put own thick roots into the soil beneath the ot. Fine, fibrous roots under the pot are othing to worry about. Check for healthy)liage – withered brownish leaves and rivelled shoots suggest neglect. Blemishes re usually indicative of pests or diseases, ind or weather damage, or mechanical jury. There should not be any plain green oots on variegated plants.

Ierbaceous perennials   Buy healthy, pot-•d specimens.

A simple timber trough sets off plants to their advantage.

Narcissus (daffodils and narcissi)   Herald spring and are too well-known for description. Check ultimate height – the range is from 4in (10cm) miniatures to 20in (50cm) giants. All are excellent on their own or mixed with spring bedding in patio planters and window-boxes. Use miniatures in sinks. Plant in autumn.

Summer bedding plants   Never buy chilled plants which have been exposed to draughts and blustery winds. Good plants are stocky and sturdy with dark-green, healthy foliage and, in the case of flowering kinds, show plenty of buds. They will have been acclimatized gradually to outdoor conditions. Pale, soft and fleshy plants are typical of those which have been brought straight out of a warm greenhouse, and these are unlikely to do well.

Spring bedding plants   Buy container grown plants. However, most wall flowers are sold with bare roots, and in this case avoid any which are excessively limp.

Bulbs   A good bulb is plump, unscarred, firm and free from moulds and mildew. Check that they are of flowering size.

Fruits   Buy certified healthy stock wherever possible. Consider the eventual size and vigour and with tree fruits, take account of pollination problems – your garden centre will advise.

ost plants have their preferences when it mes to matters of sun, shade and rooting edium (*see* Chapter 1). However, there e plenty which grow happily in all but the ost extreme conditions. No plant prefers be exposed to wind and draughts, but me are more tolerant of exposed contions than others. And when it comes to owing in containers, some are better lapted than others to accept the confined ot run and significant temperature flucations imposed upon them.

he lists of plants which follow are made up tolerant varieties which are reliable and ill adapt to all but the most inhospitable uations. And most important, they are all sily obtainable.

allflowers are reliable, brightly loured, sweetly scented spring bedding ints. Check on size – heights vary from (15cm) to 2ft (60cm).

Victorian mangles are much sought-after to originate container displays.

Spring Bedding Plants (Short Term)

Set out in autumn to bloom early in the year: *Bellis* (daisy); *Cheiranthus* (wallflower); *Myosotis* (forget-me-not); *Primula* (polyanthus and primrose); *Viola* (pansy and viola).

Bulbs and corms such as: *Anemone* 'De Caen' (anemonies); *Hyacinthus* (hyacinths); *Narcissus* (daffodils and narcissi); *Scilla*; Tulipa (tulip).

Fuchsias (summer standards)   Do not confuse with hardy border fuchsias. Standards are connoisseurs' plants when trained as approximately 4ft (1.2m) high single specimens for summer display. Pink, purple, red or white bicoloured, bell-like flowers are freely produced. Use dwarf bushy plants for summer bedding in patio containers and hanging baskets. Move all plants under cover in winter.

Summer Bedding Plants (Short Term)

Set out in early summer to bloom through to autumn (lilies are planted in autumn or spring): *Ageratum; Alyssum; Begonia semperflorens; Fuchsia; Impatiens* (busy lizzie); *Kochia* (burning bush); *Lobelia; Tagetes* (French marigolds); *Nepeta glechoma* 'Variegata'.

Bulbs: *Lilium* (various lilies); *Begonia* (tuberous).

With its variegated leaves and small purple flowers, glechoma is an extremely useful trailing, summer bedding plant for container edgings.

Trailing lobelia.

Lobelia   A reliable summer bedding plant. There are dwarf compact varieties and trailers. All are covered with tiny flowers throughout summer, and come in shades of blue, violet, red, rose, white and mauve – many have a distinctive 'eye'. Unsurpassed for edgings. Trailing varieties are best for hanging and wall baskets.

dazzling summer show of nicotiana, petunias and lobelia is inexpensive to provide.

...simachia nummularia is a good trailer ...r permanently planted containers. Its ...llow summer flowers and mid-green ...aves are most attractive.

Herbaceous Perennials for Permanent Planting

Dwarf: *Lysimachia nummularia* (creeping Jenny); *Campanula cochlearifolia* 'Cambridge Blue' (bellflower); *Silene schafta* 'Robusta' (catchfly); *Sedum spathulifolium* 'Capablanca' (stonecrop); *Potentilla tonguei* (cinquefoil).

Medium: *Bergenia* (elephant's ears); *Doronicum* (leopard's bane); *Fragaria* 'Pink

Bergenia is a hardy container plant with pink spring flowers and evergreen leaves.

This smart-looking container serves several purposes. As well as housing a herbaceous plant, it is also used as a support for climbers such as this clematis.

Topiary trained specimens in containers will always provide a talking point.

Panda' (strawberry flower); *Geum*; *Houttuynia* 'Chameleon'.

Conifers

Most conifers need some shelter from strong, cold, freezing or drying winds, and some shade from intense midday summer sun. Most blue, yellow and variegated varieties colour best in sun but are worth growing in partial shade as well.

Specimens: *Chamaecyparis lawsoniana* 'Ellwoodii' (cypress); *Juniperus communis* 'Hibernica' (juniper); *Taxus baccata* 'Standishii' (yew); *Thuja occidentalis* 'Rheingold' and 'Smaragd'.

Dwarfs: *Abies balsamea* 'Nana' (fir); *Chamaecyparis lawsoniana* 'Green Globe' and 'Minima Aurea' (cypress); *Juniperus communis* 'Blue Pygmy' (juniper); *Picea mariana* 'Nana' (spruce); *Thuja occidentalis* 'Danica'.

Broad-Leaved Trees

Betula pendula (birch); *Cotoneaster* 'Hybri-

us Pendulus' (weeping cotoneaster);
aburnum 'Vossii'; *Salix* 'Kilmarnock' (Kil-
narnock willow); *Sorbus aucuparia* (rowan).

hrubs, Climbers and Wall
lants

Medium shrubs: *Buxus sempervirens* (box);
laeagnus pungens (oleaster); *Fatsia japo-*

Fatsia japonica This evergreen shrub grows
to 4ft (1.2m) in height. Its large, deeply lobed,
glossy, dark-green leaves, heads of globular,
milky-white, mid-autumn flowers and black
winter fruits make it an eminently suitable
single tub specimen. Give winter protection
from frost and strong winds in cold areas.

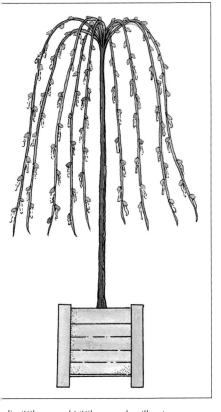

alix 'Kilmarnock' (Kilmarnock willow)
nakes an excellent specimen tree. Its
ilky-grey pussy-willow, fluffy, ball-type
atkins appear on bare stems along with
hose of a yellow pendulous habit. Mid-
reen leaves follow to provide light
ummer shade.

nica; Hydrangea macrophylla; Ligustrum
(privet); *Spiraea × bumalda; Viburnum
tinus* (winter flowering viburnum).

Dwarf shrubs: *Berberis stenophylla*
'Corallina Compacta' (barberry); *Cotoneaster dammeri* 'Streib's Findling'; *Euonymus
fortunei* varieties; *Hebe ochracea* 'James
Stirling'; *Spiraea japonica* 'Little Princess'.

Climbers and wall plants: *Chaenomeles ×
superba* (flowering quince); *Clematis* (large-
flowered); *Hedera helix* (ivy); *Jasminum*

Choisya ternata 'Sundance' (Mexican orange blossom) This 3ft (90cm) high evergreen, golden-leaved shrub carries white fragrant flowers in early summer. Makes a good focal point planted singly or in small groups. Needs protection from cold winds, winter frosts and early morning sun. The green foliage variety is hardier and taller.

For colourful autumn foliage this creeper (Parthenocissus quinquefolia, or Virginia creeper) is hard to equal.

The attractive feathery, pink flowers of Spiraea 'Little Princess' are produced over a long period, making this a container-worthy shrub.

nudiflorum (winter flowering jasmine); *Parthenocissus* (Virginia creeper).

Small Bulbs

Represent good value for money and with care will last many seasons. Permanently planted in autumn for late winter, early spring flowering: *Anemone blanda* (wind flower); *Chionodoxa lucilliae* (glory of the snow);*Crocus chrysanthus; Iris reticulata* (dwarf iris); *Muscari azureum* (grape hyacinth); *Narcissus cyclamineus* 'Jack Snipe' (dwarf narcissus); *Scilla tubergeniana* (squill).

(Opposite) Timber containers such as these can be used to great effect to grow climbing plants.

3 • EDIBLE CROPS

Fresh, home-grown fruit and vegetables are an attractive proposition. However, when grown in containers they tend to be bulky and rather untidy, so be highly selective in the choice of crops. Fruits and vegetables must be given attention as demanded, and this may mean watering several times a day during the summer. So leave these plants well alone unless there is sufficient time and enthusiasm to attend to the job properly.

The following food crops should be grown in an open, sunny spot, shaded from fierce midday sun and sheltered from cold and drying winds.

Fruits

Eating apples   Grow early, mid-season and late varieties of modern 'Ballerina'. They crop well and require minimum attention.
Soft fruits   Liquid feed every fortnight during summer.
  Blackcurrant: grow compact-bush varieties. Starting with the oldest, systematically prune out a third of the branches each autumn – down to compost level.
  Gooseberry: grow mildew resistant bush varieties. Once picking is over, shorten all side-shoots back to three leaves and cut out weak and ingrowing stems.
  Summer fruiting strawberry: plant up afresh each autumn using home-raised plants propagated by pinning down plantlets into small pots of compost during the summer.

Vegetables, Salads and Herbs

Tomato   There are two types – dwarf and tall standard. All are set out in early summer after all danger of frost has gone. Give them a warm, sunny, sheltered spot, preferably backed by a warm wall. Plant singly in 9in

There are no proper branches with this compact modern apple tree. The apples form close into the main stem.

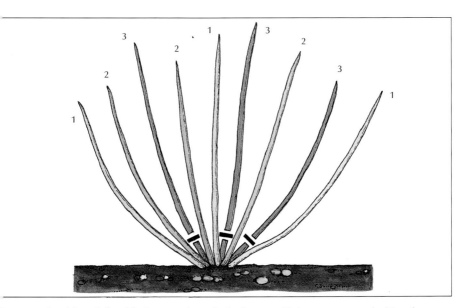

Prune out the oldest, darkest blackcurrant shoots in the first year (3). Leave new growths (1) and two-year-old shoots (2) untouched.

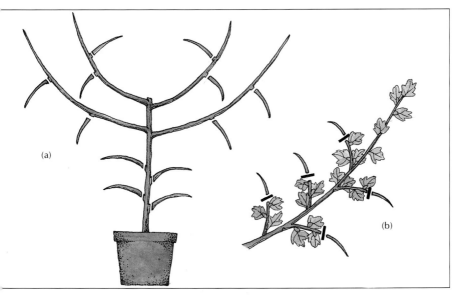

Create a bowl-shaped framework of main branches on a clear gooseberry stem. (a) Cut out ingrowing, crossing or down-growing shoots. (b) Prune side-shoots back to three leaves.

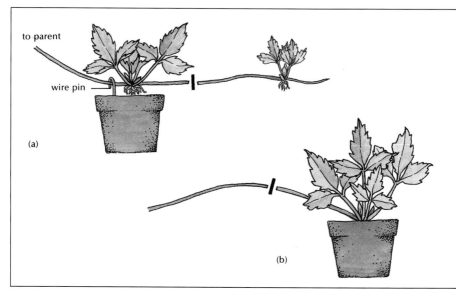

(a) Press the strawberry plantlet down on to the compost and peg in place with a wire pin. Remove other plantlets beyond this point when pegging down. (b) Sever from the parent when rooted.

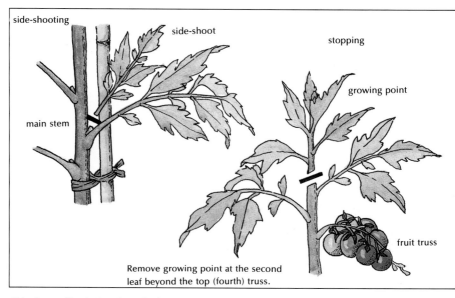

Side-shoot tall varieties of standard tomatoes to conserve the plant's energy. Remove growing points during late summer – this encourages the fruit to ripen before the onset of cold weather.

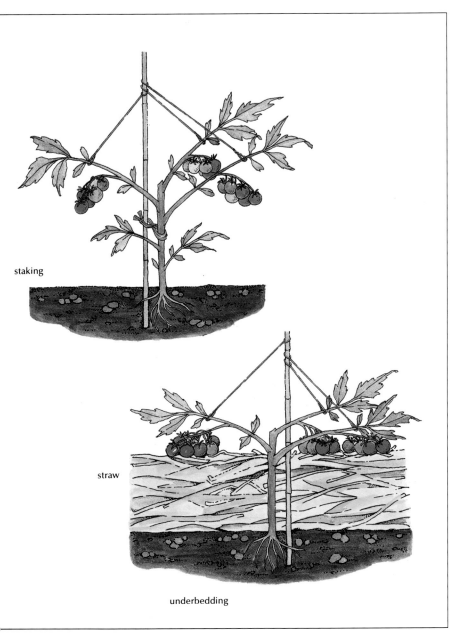

staking

straw

underbedding

Underbed bush tomatoes with straw to keep fruits clean and unblemished. Staking and tying ensures a good circulation of air.

(23cm) pots or three to a growbag. Bush varieties do well in box beds. Liquid feed weekly, starting as the first fruitlets form. Limit tall kinds to a single stem by removing side-shoots as they grow. Tie in to a support every 6in (15cm). Remove the growing point from tall kinds once the fourth truss has formed. Allow bush kinds to grow unchecked – however, they do benefit from staking

Lettuce   Sow summer maturing varieties in drills in box beds, keeping up a succession of sowings from mid-spring to mid-summer. Thin out plants when 1in (3cm) high to the spacing recommended on the seed packet. Liquid feed weekly after thinning.

Radish   Sow quick maturing, round or oval varieties thinly, in shallow drills in box beds. Sow in succession from mid-spring to late summer. Pull as soon as useable.

Salad onions   Grow 'White Lisbon' as for radish.

Beetroot   Grow quick maturing globe varieties as for radish. Thin when about 1in (3cm) high and harvest immediately the are useable. Leaves must be twisted off and never cut.

Carrot   Grow quick maturing round varieties as for radish.

French beans   Sow six seeds around the edge of an 8in (20cm) pot. Keep up succession from mid-spring to mid summer. Support with twiggy pieces of stic pushed into the compost amongst the plants. Liquid feed weekly once the firs pods have formed. Pick when the beans are young.

Salad potatoes   (Pink Fir Apples and Ratte)   In mid-spring, bury two tubers pe 10in (25cm) pot which is half-filled with potting compost. Top up with more com post as growth is made. Liquid feed weekl once the plants are in flower.

Mixed herbs   Plant up a mixed herb ba rel (*see* page 42). Perennial herbs like balm hyssop, sage, thyme, mint and chives ar on sale throughout the year. Short-term

First thinning – to 5in (13cm) apart.   Second thinning – remove or use alternate plants.

Thin lettuce promptly to avoid overcrowding, otherwise the crop may run prematurely to seed.

Sow in dibber holes.

Pull when on the young side and twist off the foliage. If beet are cut, the colour will drain away.

Herbs like basil, borage, fennel, parsley and savory are planted in late spring and grubbed out when picking is over.

French beans crop well when grown in containers.

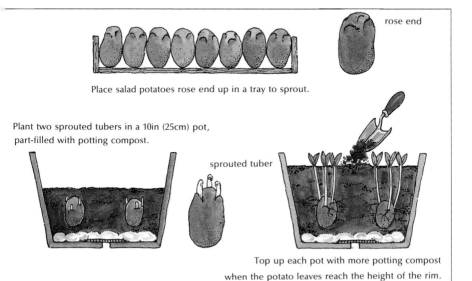

rose end

Place salad potatoes rose end up in a tray to sprout.

Plant two sprouted tubers in a 10in (25cm) pot, part-filled with potting compost.

sprouted tuber

Top up each pot with more potting compost when the potato leaves reach the height of the rim.

Salad potatoes are a luxury vegetable well suited to container growing. Top up with potting compost as the potatoes grow.

4 • PREPARATION

Potting Composts

Since container plants depend on obtaining all their nutrients and moisture from a limited root run, potting composts are of prime importance. Garden soil should not be used in containers. It tends to pan down, offers poor drainage, contains few nutrients and can be contaminated with pest and disease organisms. Most branded proprietary potting composts make good moisture-retentive, airy, open-textured, nutritional, crumbly rooting mediums. Traditionally there are two types – soil-based and peat-based.

Rosa (roses)   When in bloom, roses are unequalled for their scent and beauty. Bush and standard roses are best planted singly in patio containers – but only move them into prominent positions when actually in flower. Group plant miniatures into largish containers. Climbers are useful for covering trellis, walls and fencing.

Container plants and statuary can create an interesting scene, as here.

Soil-based composts   These are balanced mixtures of sterilized soil, peat, sand and other aggregate plus fertilizer and ground limestone. They are ideal for most container crops, but are essential for long-stay plants which are going to be left undisturbed for six months or longer. They give good anchorage and support, are easy to manage and retain their physical qualities well. They are fairly heavy and so there is little risk of free-standing containers blowing over.

Peat-based composts   These contain n▪ soil. The other components are balanced u▪ accordingly and anchorage and support ar▪ only fair. They hold too much water i▪ winter and dry out over-rapidly on a ho▪ summer's day. Once dry they are extremel▪ difficult to wet again. These are lightweigh▪ composts and are ideal for hanging an▪ wall baskets.

Modern proprietary 50:50 potting compos▪ are made up of equal parts of soil and pea▪ based mixtures. They combine the best o▪

These stone troughs are ideal for creating a mini rockery, though they might be expensive to purchase.

This trough houses a fine collection of mixed saxifrage.

Purple violas contrast well with grey foliage in this hanging basket.

Tulipa (tulips)   Tulips come in a wide range of heights, shapes, forms and colours. Use early flowering kinds for spring bedding, otherwise they may not have flowered in time to plant up with summer bedding. Relate plant height to the container. Tulips are impressive when massed on their own or mixed with the likes of forget-me-nots.

both worlds and can be used with confidence for most jobs.

Lime-free composts should be used for rhododendrons, camellias, azaleas and heathers, along with other plants that are intolerant of lime.

Choosing Containers

- Relate the cost to likely container life.
- Don't skimp on size, but the size must be related to the plants (*see* Chapter 1). Shrubs and trees will eventually need containers of 14in (35cm) to 2ft (60cm) in diameter (*see* pages 38 and 47). The best sizes for hanging baskets are 10in (25cm) and 12in (30cm).
- Ensure that there are sufficient drainage holes in the base of all containers or you will risk winter waterlogging.
- Check for top heaviness or risk instability. Lightweight, free-standing plastic containers depend on the weight of compost for stability and should always be filled with soil-based mixtures.
- Containers which narrow at the top are difficult to handle when repotting.

wall planter

window-box

hanging basket

urn

tub or planter

sink

terracotta pot

patio planter

pool container

barrel tub or planter

Choose a container suited to the job in hand.

A colour grouping of uncommon container plants seen in France.

This colourful, if slightly overpowering, pair of hanging baskets has been used to flank a doorway.

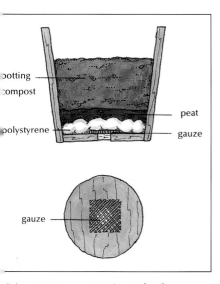

*is important to pay attention to detail
when preparing a container for planting.*

Poorly insulated, lightweight plastic containers are best reserved for summer crops. They offer little root protection, and they may burst if the compost freezes – this is also the case with many terracotta and ceramic pots.

Use straight-backed containers for planting climbers and wall plants.

Solid-sided hanging baskets are easier to plant and handle than the traditional wire varieties. Check they are fitted with drip trays. Convert wire baskets to solid-sided types by inserting fibre liners.

Check supports on hanging baskets – modern snap-on hangers are less secure than chains.

Preparing a Patio Container

Disinfect all 'used' containers. Soak all new porous terracotta, concrete and reconstituted stone containers for twenty-four hours in clean water before filling.

*Almost any container can be made watertight
with the use of a flexible pool liner.*

● If re-using old containers, take particular care to clean and disinfect all cracks and crevices – they harbour pests and diseases.

● Insert a fibre liner if used. Liners are good – they increase insulation, make repotting easier and prolong the life of timber containers.

● Make drainage holes in the base of the liner. Fix gauze or fine mesh netting securely over the drainage holes. This prevents pests gaining entry from below. Bottom out the container with broken pieces of polystyrene for drainage. Cover this with a minimum ½in (1cm) layer of moist peat before filling with suitable compost, ready for planting.

Round terracotta pots liven up the grey paving and wall, and soften the straight lines and angles of this patio.

Preparing a Free-Standing Pool Container

● The size of the container is important. A minimum depth of 12in (30cm) is needed for aquatic plants – miniature water lilies apart, they will grow in 3in (8cm) of water. A depth of 18in (45cm) is needed if fish are included. Within reason, the larger the surface area of water, the easier the pool is to manage, and overcrowding is less of problem.

● Make the container watertight by bun ing up the drainage holes, taking care n to leave any rough internal edges. Lir the container with a proprietary, flexib pool liner and secure this into place aroun the inside of the rim with a suitable fi ative. Once it has set, fill with rain- or ta water, provided it has not passed through

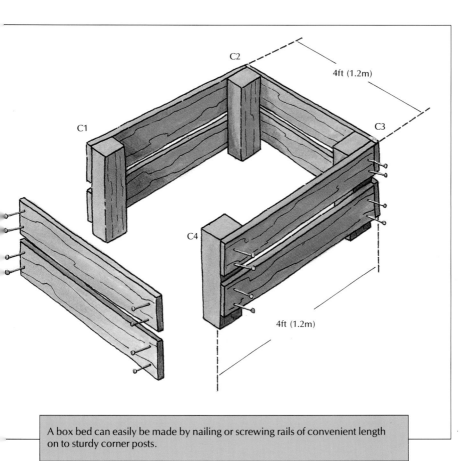

C2

4ft (1.2m)

C1

C3

C4

4ft (1.2m)

A box bed can easily be made by nailing or screwing rails of convenient length on to sturdy corner posts.

omestic water softener. Allow to stand for few days before introducing plants or fish.

Water attracts young children, and any zeable container should be covered over ›curely with an open-mesh grill.

⁄laking a Box Bed

Box beds are raised beds. They are ideal ⁊r growing vegetables, salads, herbs, fruits ⁊d cut flowers on the patio when they are ›sitioned in a sheltered spot away from the ⁊ips of buildings and trees. The more

ornate box beds are well suited for decorative displays.

● A basic box bed: aim to construct a bottomless box of 4ft (1.2m) square and a minimum 9in (23cm) deep. Use two 4in × 1in × 4ft (10cm × 3cm × 1.2m) timber rails for each side of the box. They are fixed on to 2in × 1in × 10in (5cm × 3cm × 25cm) corner timbers – one on top of the other with a 1in (3cm) gap between. Treat with a safe horticultural preservative before filling.

● Ornate box beds can be constucted from brick or architectural blocks.

5 • PLANTING UP

Potting Up a New Specimen Tree or Shrub

● Select a container which is one or two sizes larger than the existing one and prepare it for potting (*see* page 35). Water the plant thoroughly and allow it to drain for an hour before removing the pot. Take a pointed stick and poke out the old drainage materials along with any loose compost. Trim back any damaged roots and then stand the exposed rootball inside the prepared container. Remove or add potting compost so that the top of the rootball is about ¾in (2cm) below the rim. Spread out any of the outermost roots which are free and work moist compost around the rootball, gently firming as filling proceeds. Fill to within ½in (1cm) of the rim, leaving a space for watering. Finally, water to settle the compost. Shelter from wind and sun for a few days.

Planting Up a Sink

● Use a sink with a minimum depth of 6in (15cm). Raise it up on blocks and slide drip tray beneath. Then prepare for planting (*see* page 35).
● Planting ideas: rock and alpine plant displays; miniature heather and slow growing conifers; succulents for sun; ferns for shade; and herbs.
● Plunge-plant by setting out plants complete with their pots and buried up to their rims in compost. This method enables plants of differing growth rates and soil preferences to be included. Shorter term plants can be lifted out without disturbing the longer term ones, and when replanting plants are easy to deal with. The growth rate of the more vigorous specimens can be controlled by repotting (*see* page 47). Part bury pieces of rock amongst rock and alpine plants.

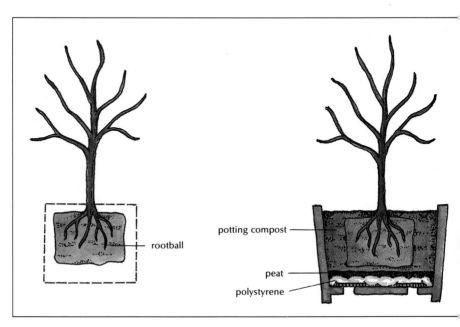

Set the tree or shrub centrally with its best side facing the main viewing point.

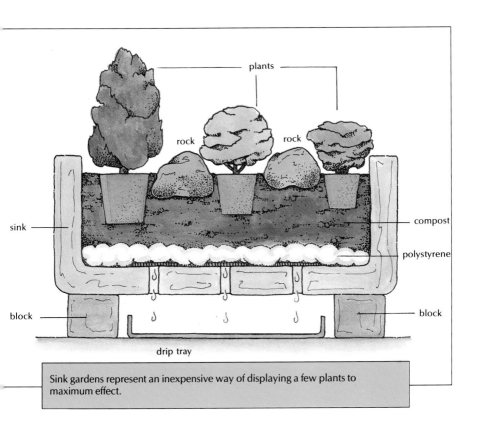

Sink gardens represent an inexpensive way of displaying a few plants to maximum effect.

Planting Up a Window-Box

Use a box with a minimum depth and width of 7in (18cm), with drainage holes in the base and a drip tray beneath. Prepare for planting (*see* page 35). Spring bedding followed by summer bedding is popular (*see* pages 11, 16 and 17–20). Most compact varieties of spring bedding and bulbs are suitable – bellis, polyanthus and winter pansies will flower spasmodically during winter. Most smaller summer bedding are fine, provided they are matched to the site.

Permanent displays of rock plants, small bulbs, miniature conifers and trailing ivies can be plunge-planted in spring (*see* page 38).

● Set taller plants to the back, more dwarfing kinds to the front and edge round the sides and front with trailers. Use soil-based compost for all overwintering displays.

Planting Up a Free-Standing Patio Container

● A succession of bedding is popular – as with window-boxes.
● Containers viewed from all sides are treated like the top of a hanging basket, but with plants in scale with container size. Allow the centre tall plant – or group of plants – to cover about a third of the total surface area. In larger containers try plunge-

A simple yet stunning sink garden in spring.

A continental style arrangement of marigolds, geraniums and fuchsias taken in France.

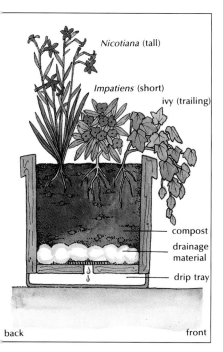

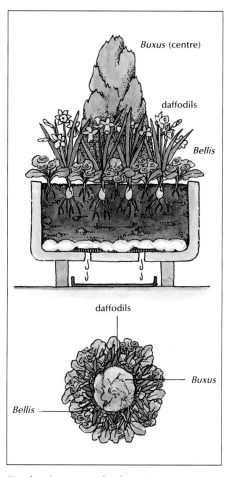

*Window-boxes are designed to take
smaller plants. At no time should they
reach more than a third of the way up the
window, otherwise they may obstruct too
much light.*

planting an evergreen dwarf shrub or conifer centrally, to give height and save on
bedding.

In front-facing containers, set tall plants
at the back with infillers to grade plants
down to a front edging on three sides.
Plants at the back should have a maximum
ultimate height of about three times the
depth of the container. Here, too, savings
can be made by plunge-planting one or two
evergreen shrubs or conifers (*see* page 38).

Planting Up a Solid-Sided Hanging Basket

Plant up as soon as summer bedding

*Simple schemes are often best. Here an
evergreen* Buxus *is plunge-planted
centrally and then surrounded with
daffodils and bellis for a spring display.*

plants become available. Then give the
basket indoor protection at night until all
risk of frost has past. Only then hang it
outdoors.

● Bottom out the basket with broken
pieces of polystyrene and part-fill with
moist potting compost (*see* page 35). Use a
lightweight peat-based mix to which a few

pieces of charcoal have been added to keep it sweet. Plant a tall, bushy or spiky plant centrally – kochia, geranium, fuchsia and tall begonias are good plants. Surround the centre plant with more dwarfing infillers like geraniums, busy Lizzies, begonias, French marigolds, pansies and ageratum. Edge around with trailers like lobelia, ivy, glechoma and trailing geraniums to cascade over the edge.

Planting Up a Herb Pot or Strawberry Barrel

● Gauze over the drainage holes and bottom out with polystyrene (*see* page 35). Then, if using a model without a 'built-in' watering tube, make provision for watering by building up a central core of coarse gravel in a wire netting tube. The tube should reach from the bottom to the top of

This mixed planting includes spring flowering bulbs and provides a strong focal point.

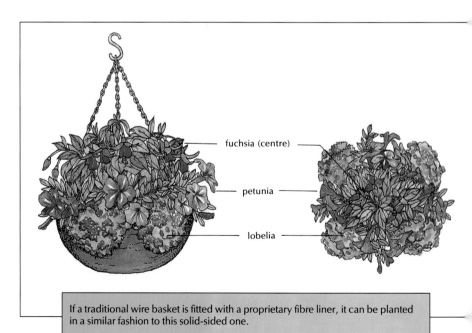

fuchsia (centre)

petunia

lobelia

If a traditional wire basket is fitted with a proprietary fibre liner, it can be planted in a similar fashion to this solid-sided one.

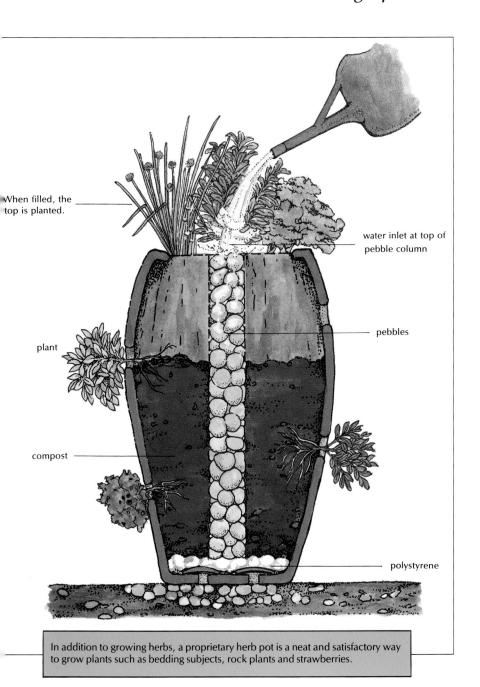

When filled, the top is planted.

water inlet at top of pebble column

pebbles

plant

compost

polystyrene

In addition to growing herbs, a proprietary herb pot is a neat and satisfactory way to grow plants such as bedding subjects, rock plants and strawberries.

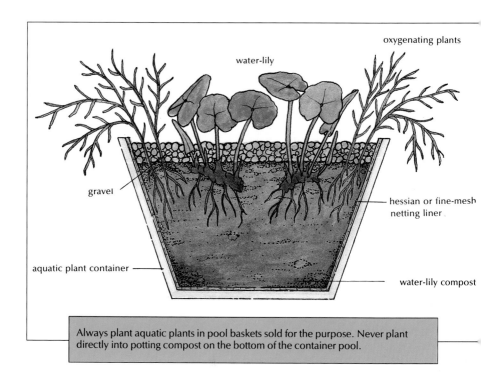

oxygenating plants

water-lily

gravel

hessian or fine-mesh netting liner

aquatic plant container

water-lily compost

Always plant aquatic plants in pool baskets sold for the purpose. Never plant directly into potting compost on the bottom of the container pool.

the barrel. Subsequently, water is poured down the gravel tube and seeps through to the plants. With the tube in position, part-fill the barrel with soil-based potting compost – level with the bottom planting hole. Feed a plant through from the outside, and, with the roots well spread out, pack in more compost, bringing the level up to the second hole. Insert another plant and then continue thus, alternating plants with compost until the last planting hole has been filled. Finally plant up to the top.

Planting Up a Container Pool

● Prepare a pool container (*see* page 36). The initial choice of plants and livestock is vital. Opt for professionally selected minia-ture pool collections of both plants and fish.

Plant in late spring in proprietary baskets, fitted with liners and filled with proprietary water-lily compost. Insert a sachet of pool fertilizer. Rinse plants in clean water, then plant as instructed on the label. After plant-ing, top over the soil with chippings. Position planted baskets at the correct depth in the pool container – as instructed on the label. The depth is measured from the top of the soil in the basket. The baskets needing the least depth are stood on bricks. 'Floaters' are an exception – this group of plants is simply dropped on to the water surface. Immediately after planting, expect some cloudiness: this should clear in a few weeks.

Planting Up a Growbag

● Filled with peat-based composts, pro

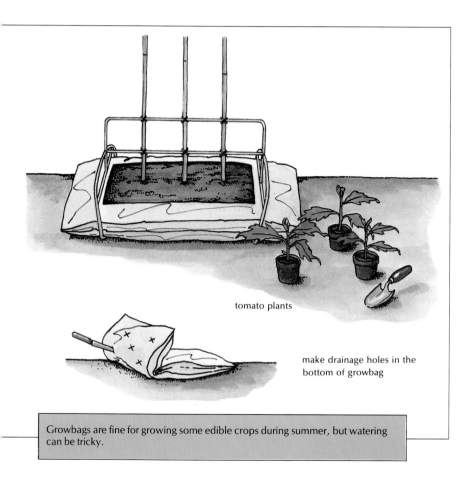

tomato plants

make drainage holes in the bottom of growbag

Growbags are fine for growing some edible crops during summer, but watering can be tricky.

rietary growbags are popular, widely used nd well suited to short-term crops like omatoes and lettuces which are grown utdoors during the summer.

Cut drainage holes in the base of each rowbag before removing the top according the maker's instructions. Before planting, nsure that the compost is thoroughly moist nd sufficient of it is exposed to allow for a ee circulation of air. Don't worry if the ompost turns green at the surface. Use roprietary growbag supports for the likes of andard tomatoes – they are the only really atisfactory means of support.

● Never attempt to re-use a growbag a second season, although the contents need not be wasted as they make an excellent mulch for border plants.

Sowing Salads and Vegetables in a Box Bed

● Having positioned the box (*see* page 37), bottom out with 1½in (4cm) of washed gravel topped over with 1in (3cm) of coarse peat. Then fill up to the top with soil-based potting compost. Use the back of a rake to

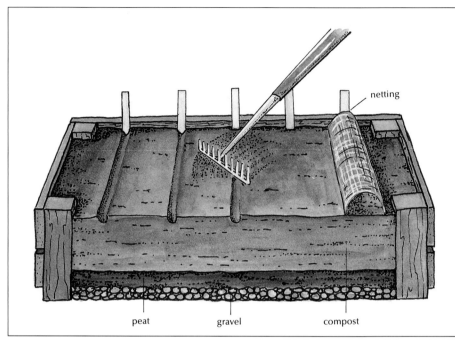

netting

peat   gravel   compost

Box beds are well suited for growing salads, vegetables and annual flowers for cutting – these crops are sown direct and thinned. Yields are also good when planted up with the likes of strawberries, herbs and bush tomatoes.

take out a shallow furrow alongside a taut line to the depth specified on the seed packet. If the compost is dry, water the bottom of the drill and allow the water to seep in before sowing. Sow thinly and rake compost over the seeds, then lightly firm by tamping with the back of the rake. Mark and label the rows and protect from birds with pegged-down netting.

● Each spring, treat the existing compost with a horticultural disinfectant before topping up with more fresh compost. The original filling will then last for many years.

When choosing containers, take into account the colour of both foliage and flowers. Contrast between pot and plant can be most effective.

Potting On and Repotting Trees and Shrubs

Potting on involves moving plants into progressively larger containers over a period of years – annually, in either autumn or spring. This keeps them healthy and encourages them to make further steady growth. Potting (*see* page 38).

Repotting – most trees and shrubs eventually reach a size when it is unwise to encourage them to grow anymore. Repotting back into the same-sized container keeps them healthy and restricts their growth. Repotting in alternate years or one year in three is the norm. The procedure is slightly more drastic than potting up new stock (*see* page 38). Poke out as much of the old compost as possible and reduce rootball size by cutting the roots back by up to one-fifth before repotting. Top-dress in the intervening years.

Top-Dressing

• On average, permanent containerized plants are repotted every other year. In the interim they need to be top-dressed. Potting compost enriched with a balanced fertilizer such as Growmore makes an excellent top-dressing. Add 4oz (112g) of Growmore to each 2 gallon (9 litre) bucketful of standard soil-based potting compost. Mix thoroughly and moisten. Top-dressings are applied in spring as a matter of routine just as the plants are starting into growth. Then, if there is any significant loss through rain-

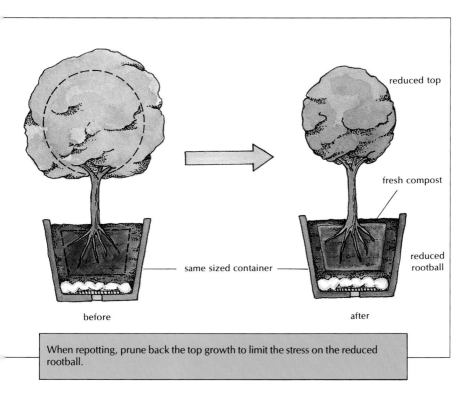

reduced top

fresh compost

same sized container

reduced rootball

before

after

When repotting, prune back the top growth to limit the stress on the reduced rootball.

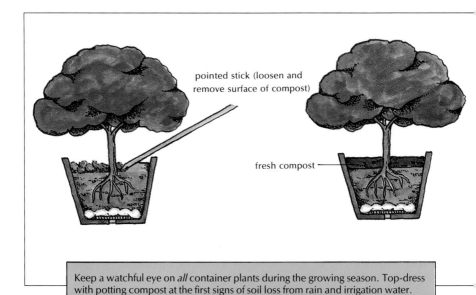

pointed stick (loosen and remove surface of compost)

fresh compost

Keep a watchful eye on *all* container plants during the growing season. Top-dress with potting compost at the first signs of soil loss from rain and irrigation water.

An Agapanthus, *or African lily, stands in the foreground.*

or irrigation water, they are replenished during the growing season and topped up in autumn. Take a pointed stick and prick to loosen up any surface crust before scraping away the top 1in (3cm) or so of old compost, together with all traces of weed and moss. Water thoroughly, then top up with the moist-enriched potting compost.

Watering

● Collect rain-water in butts via gutters and downspouts. This ensures a supply in times of restrictions.

● Using a can with a fine rose, or a hose with adjustable spray attachment, apply water gently on to the compost surface. Don't splash the foliage in bright sunlight or you will risk scorch. Continue watering until any surplus water trickles out at the bottom of the container. Ensure it isn't just running down between the rootball and the sides of the container, as happens if the

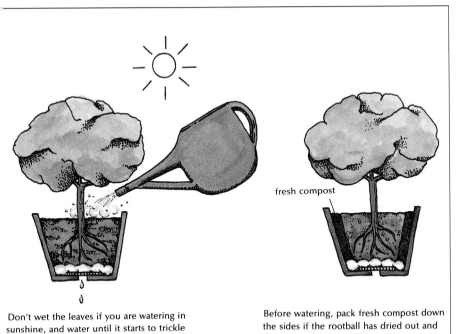

Don't wet the leaves if you are watering in sunshine, and water until it starts to trickle out at the bottom.

Before watering, pack fresh compost down the sides if the rootball has dried out and shrunk from the container.

More plants are lost through faulty watering than any other single cause.

ompost has dried and shrunk. In this vent, pack with moist compost to fill the ap and water again. Water daily during ummer, or twice daily in excessively varm, dry or windy weather when overead spraying first thing in the morning or the evening is also beneficial. Watering ne ground around containers to increase ne humidity is also beneficial. Aim to water lants before they wilt. Watering once or vice a month during late autumn and vinter may be adequate.

eeding

Only feed actively growing plants. iquid feeds are ideal (*see* page 63), and

Liquid feed actively growing plants and avoid wetting the foliage.

you should use them from spring to early autumn – with permanent plants this is in addition to spring top-dressings. Stick to an all-purpose complete fertilizer, mix and use according to the maker's instructions. Using a can with rose attachment, water the feed on to moist compost and continue until any surplus runs out at the bottom of the container. Feed early in the day, or early in the evening provided plants are given time to dry off before nightfall. Frequent aplications are necessary. Feed salads, quick maturing vegetables and short-term bedding plants weekly, along with berry fruits and tomatoes once the fruit has set. Roses benefit from fortnightly feeds, as do fruit trees once the fruit has set. Monthly feeds during the height of the season will sustain ornamental trees and shrubs. Camellias, magnolias and rhododendrons are exceptions – top dressings are sufficient.

Staking and Tying Ornamentals

● When dealing with standard trees obtain a timber stake which is as thick a the stem of the tree and long enough t reach to within 2–3in (3–5cm) of the lowe branches when in position. After repottin the tree, hammer home the stake close int the stem. Then secure stem to stake wit two proprietary tree ties complete wit spacers. Fit one near the top and the othe half-way down. Omit the spacers and yo will risk chafed bark and strangulatio Basal branching trees and bushes ar treated very much as for standards – allo

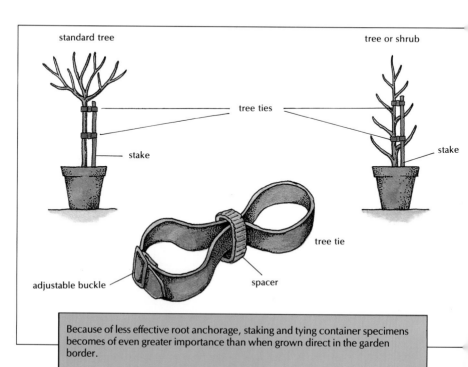

Because of less effective root anchorage, staking and tying container specimens becomes of even greater importance than when grown direct in the garden border.

the stake for each to reach about two-thirds the way up the tree or bush.

● Lightweight split or metal canes are suitable for supporting individual soft-stemmed plants when pushed into the compost close to the plant. Use proprietary plant ties to secure the stem every 5in (12cm). Proprietary hoop supports and link stakes are excellent for keeping multi-stemmed plants in place. Use as the makers direct.

Supporting a Wall-Trained Climber

● A Trellis is ideal for training most climbers. Trellises are available in variously shaped panels, mostly in plastic-coated metal or timber. Opt for the best type for the job in hand. Aim to have the trellis in place before positioning the container (a flat-backed container is best). Most plastic panels come complete with spacers and screws – erect as the makers direct. One good way of fixing a timber trellis is to screw it to a batten frame of 1in (3cm) minimum thickness. Then fix the assembled unit to the wall by screwing into previously drilled and plugged holes. By securing the trellis at least 1in (3cm) out from the wall, a good circulation of air is ensured. This prevents moisture being trapped between the wall and climber and so there is little risk of penetrating damp. In addition, any aerial roots are kept away from the

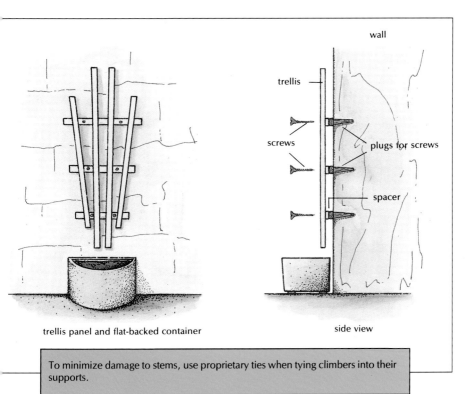

trellis panel and flat-backed container

side view

To minimize damage to stems, use proprietary ties when tying climbers into their supports.

Thin out overcrowded pool plants, but leave two-thirds of the surface covered with foliage.

masonry, where in time they could cause damage – old masonry is most at risk.

Miniature Pool Care

● Algae are the scourge of garden pools. These tiny plants thrive in sunlight, feed on mineral salts, cause greening and completely take over ponds. Pool care is geared towards starving algae of sunlight and food. If pool plants make excessive growth during summer, thin them out, but always aim to have at least two-thirds but no more of the pool surface covered with vegetation. This deprives the algae of sufficient sunlight for rampant growth. As organic matter decays, mineral salts are released into the water, so aim to keep the pool clear of fallen leaves and decaying vegetation at all times. When feeding plants, use only proprietary pool sachets a general fertilizers increase the mineral salts Pool plants are normally only fed annually when repotted. Fish need to be fed from spring to autumn when they go into a natural fast. Only give what food can be consumed by the fish in five minutes, otherwise the remainder drops to the bottom decays and increases the mineral salt content of the water. If aphids and other pest are in evidence, gently push the leave under water and weight them down – the fish will devour the insects. Very small

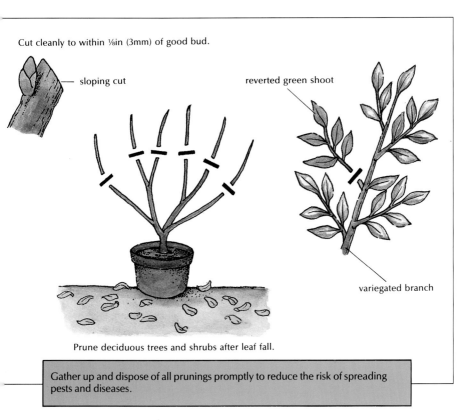

Cut cleanly to within ⅛in (3mm) of good bud.

sloping cut

reverted green shoot

variegated branch

Prune deciduous trees and shrubs after leaf fall.

Gather up and dispose of all prunings promptly to reduce the risk of spreading pests and diseases.

container pools will need emptying and cleaning out annually, in either autumn or spring.

General Routine Pruning

Consult a good pruning manual for matters of detail.

• When pruning, always cut back cleanly to within ⅛in (3mm) of a good outward pointing bud – or flush with a vigorous shoot or main stem – sloping the cut away from the bud. Paint any wounds over ¾in (2cm) diameter with a proprietary sealing preparation.

• Prune deciduous trees and shrubs in autumn after leaf fall. Conifers and broad-leaved evergreens need little pruning. When required, deal with them in late spring or summer.

• Cut out any dead, diseased or damaged stems hard back to the sound tissue as soon as you see them. Also cut out or shorten back crossing, inward growing or straggly, weak and misplaced shoots as a matter of routine (this is called sanitation pruning). Reverted green shoots should be cut out of variegated plants – if left untouched they will, in time, smother out the variegated variety. Shorten back the shoots of bush roses by a third of their length in autumn and then cut them hard back to three buds in spring.

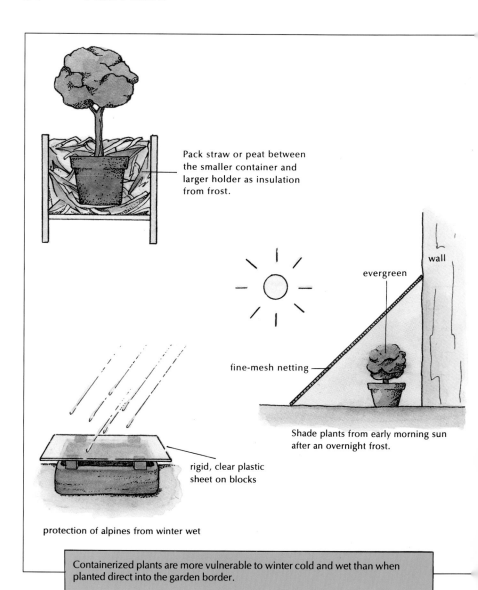

Pack straw or peat between the smaller container and larger holder as insulation from frost.

wall

evergreen

fine-mesh netting

Shade plants from early morning sun after an overnight frost.

rigid, clear plastic sheet on blocks

protection of alpines from winter wet

Containerized plants are more vulnerable to winter cold and wet than when planted direct into the garden border.

Overwintering

● In exposed gardens, erect or grow a permeable windscreen of 6ft (1.8m) mini-mum height to protect plants. Use hedging, open-work fencing or architectural blocks. Similarly, block off the ends between build-ings to reduce wind tunnelling effects. In old winter areas, pot trees and shrubs into inner containers. Stand these inside much larger outer containers and fill the spaces between the two with straw or peat to give frost protection to roots.

Scorched leaves, shoots and buds are likely if frozen plants thaw out quickly in early morning sun. Shade all frozen plants with netting until they have thawed.

Sinks of rock and alpine plants are at risk from rain and hail – protect them with a sheet of rigid plastic rested on corner pegs and weighted down. Keep a check on all drip trays – they can fill with water. No plant should be left standing in water.

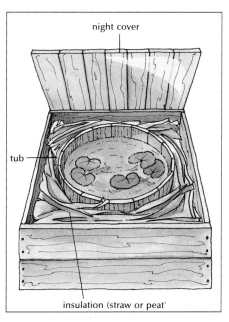

Ensure a watchful eye is kept on pool plants and fish when they are moved into their winter quarters.

Overwintering a Miniature Pool, Plants and Fish

● Where the container is small enough to move, transfer it in its entirety into a well-lit, cool shed or garage. Don't allow the water to freeze or the fish will suffer and the container may crack. Insulate the container as necessary, cover the top overnight in prolonged severe weather and uncover it to ventilate it in the warmth of the day.

● If the container is too large to man-handle, buy an 'overwintering' container and position this under cover as above. Part-fill with water taken from the existing container, dropping the level down by two-thirds. Then transfer fish plus plants complete with their baskets into their winter quarters. Pick over plants to remove decaying foliage. Finally, top up with fresh

Variegated ivy.

Hedera (hardy outdoor ivies) These climbing or trailing, self-clinging permanent foliage plants are easy to grow. They look well trailing down from hanging baskets, window-boxes and other patio containers, and are excellent trained over trellis and other supports to give year-round interest. Clip back to restrain into their allotted space.

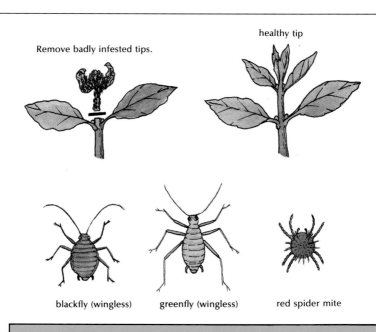

Remove badly infested tips.

healthy tip

blackfly (wingless)   greenfly (wingless)   red spider mite

Greenflies, blackflies and red spider mites must be dealt with in the early stages of an attack if they are not to get out of hand.

feeding

watering

potting

pruning

overcrowding

climate

siting

training

staking

pests

diseases

weeds

Aim to pinpoint and remedy the main causes of any signs of unthriftiness.

water. If the fish remain active when under cover, continue feeding during winter. Empty the patio container and clean it out.

Pests

● Greenfly, blackfly, ants and red spiders are the most common container pests. Colonizing around soft growth tips, greenfly and blackfly are known to most gardeners. Ants, too, are familiar. However, some may have problems identifying red spiders, especially in the early stages. These minute reddish or yellowish mites are diffcult to see with the naked eye. As they feed on leaf undersides and flowers they envelop the plant with extremely fine webbing. In advanced attacks, expect a mottling and bronzing of leaves, stunted growth and dull flowers. Red spiders thrive in the warm conditions created when container plants are grown against warm walls. Increasing humidity by wetting the ground around containers during the day and watering plants overhead in the evening during warm weather helps to keep red spiders in check. Combat greenfly and blackfly by cutting out severely infested shoots.

Trouble-Shooting Check-list

● In recognizing a plant's malaise it is most important to isolate any contributory causes which may have weakened plants and made them vulnerable to pest and disease attack.

● Consider climatic factors and the siting of plants, and are the plants overcrowded?

● Check containers — are they the right size, are they well drained, and have the drainage holes been covered with gauze to prevent the entry of soil pests?

● Has lime-free compost been used for acid lovers, for example? If not, unthriftiness

A profusion of containers, tiered for effect, and a small piece of statuary, create an oasis of peace and tranquility.

and a yellowing of the leaves is almost inevitable.

● Review cultivations — are potting, feeding, watering and pruning up to standard? More container plants die from too much or too little water than from any other single cause.

● What about general management and hygiene? Are plants picked over regularly to remove dead or diseased flowers, leaves and shoots? Are the weeds removed promptly from standing areas in and around containers? Are containers disinfected before re-use?

7 • SEASON BY SEASON

Spring

- Increase watering – every other day may suffice (*see* page 48).
- Top-dress permanent plants (*see* page 47).
- Dead-head plants.
- Pot on or repot permanent plants, pool plants included (*see* page 47).
- Buy in and pot up new stock (*see* page 38).
- Plant up pool containers (*see* page 44).
- Make first sowings in box beds of salads and vegetables (*see* pages 45–6).
- Start off salad potatoes (*see* page 28).
- Start feeding fish (*see* page 52).
- Harden off bought in summer bedding plants (*see* page 63).
- Prune out blackened, frosted shoots back to sound wood, and attend to sanitation pruning (*see* page 53).

A proprietary fish-feeding ring reduces waste and contamination.

Geraniums and impatiens provide a riot of colour in this balcony garden.

blackened, frosted tips are not pruned
ack to sound wood, they will soon die
ght back into the heart of the plant.

ummer

Water containers daily, or twice daily
uring warm, dry or windy weather (*see*
age 48).

Liquid feed following manufacturer's
uide-lines (*see* pages 49–50).

Pick over and dead-head plants, remov-
g dead and diseased foliage and faded
owers. Do not remove faded flowers
here berries are required.

Clip evergreens to shape where necess-
y.

Cut back evergreen climbers such as ivy
confine them to their allotted space.

Summer prune large-flowered clematis
y cutting weak side-shoots back to two
aves.

See to sanitation pruning (*see* page 53).

Thin out pool plants and give a general
ean up as necessary (*see* page 52). Feed
h.

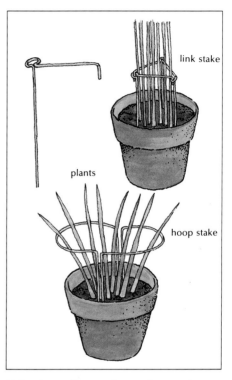

*Link stakes and hoop stakes neatly support
multi-stemmed plants.*

*These bright petunias ('Picotee Mixed')
will strike a cheerful note in summer.*

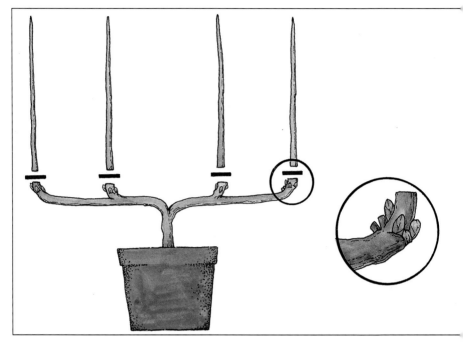

If large-flowered clematis are not pruned in autumn, they will soon deteriorate. Prune back flowered stems to within three buds of the main framework.

● Keep standing areas free of weeds.
● Cut out any shoots which are badly infested with greenfly or blackfly (*see* page 57).
● Set out short-term summer bedding plants in early summer (*see* pages 11, 16 and 17–20).
● Buy in and pot up tender plants like tomatoes.
● Make succession sowings of salads and vegetables.
● Stake and tie plants as required and as they grow (*see* pages 50–1).

Autumn

● Decrease watering – one day in three perhaps (*see* pages 48–9).
● Reduce liquid feeds – nothing after mid-autumn (*see* pages 49–50).
● Top-dress containers of permanent plants where the levels of compost have fallen (*see* page 47).
● Feed fish well to build up reserves before they go into their natural fast.
● Pick over plants, removing dead and diseased foliage.
● See to sanitation pruning (*see* page 53).
● Prune deciduous trees if necessary.
● Prune all large-flowered clematis side shoots back to within three buds of the main frame.
● Remove fallen leaves from pools.
● Prepare plants and pools for winter (*see* pages 54–7).
● Check stakes and ties.
● Set out spring bedding plants and spring flowering bulbs.

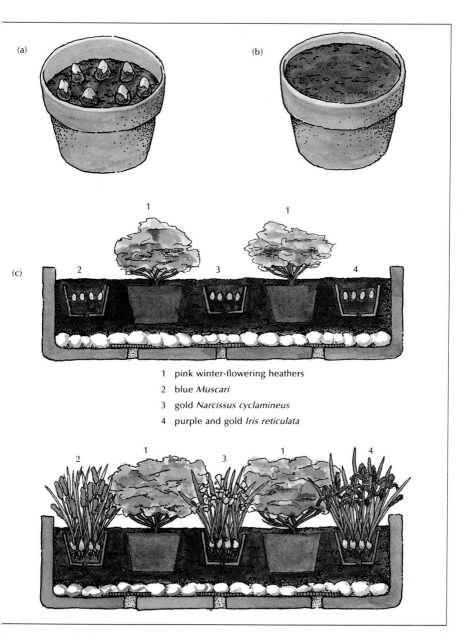

(a)

(b)

(c)

1 pink winter-flowering heathers
2 blue *Muscari*
3 gold *Narcissus cyclamineus*
4 purple and gold *Iris reticulata*

Potting up small bulbs. (b) Pot ready for plunge-planting. (c) Window-box plunge-planted
with: 1 heathers (winter flowering); 2 Muscari; 3 (dwarf narcissi); 4 dwarf iris. All the bulbs
are now in flower.

Polyanthus mixed with myosotis.

Polyanthus These are popular and unequalled when used as spring flowering bedding plants in window-boxes and patio containers. Their large, bright and cheerful single primrose-like flowers come in many colours and are carried in clustered heads. Either mass polyanthus on their own or mix them with other spring bedding plants and bulbs.

temporary plastic cover

container

All covers must be removed regularly to allow for a free circulation of air.

● Pot up, pot on and repot permanent plants – delay until spring in cold climate areas.

Winter

● Only water when the compost is dry and never when it is frozen.

A patio makes an ideal setting for container plants. Evergreens will ensure colour year-round.

● Keep a constant check on stakes and ties.
● Cover over the tops of containers with plastic sheeting if waterlogging seems likely during prolonged wet weather.
● Empty drip trays as necessary to avoid flooding.
● Shade frozen plants with netting until they have thawed – particularly those on east-facing sites which are exposed to early morning sun. It is a quick thaw which does the damage.
● Feed fish if they remain active in pools or containers moved indoors.
● Assess the garden; plan and work out schemes, ready for implementation in spring.

GLOSSARY

Butt   This is a container used for collecting rain-water. It should have a tight fitting lid in the interests of safety and cleanliness, and a tap at the bottom for ease of withdrawal.

Conifer   A collective name for a group of trees and shrubs. They vary in height from forest giants to dwarf miniatures. Most are evergreen and cone bearing.

Deciduous   These plants drop their foliage annually – usually in autumn.

Evergreen   These plants retain their foliage throughout the year.

Hardening off   This refers to the gradual acclimatization of bought-in summer bedding plants to outdoor conditions. The best way to achieve this is to leave the plants outdoors for a longer period each day until eventually they can be left out overnight in safety.

Herbaceous plants   These are non-woody, or soft-stemmed plants. In gardening circles the term herbaceous plants is used loosely to describe rock and border perennials.

Liquid feeds   These are concentrated fertilizers which are available in powder or liquid form. They must be diluted and used strictly as per the maker's instructions.

Perennial plants   These are permanent plants which have a life expectancy of several years.

Polystyrene   The type used today as commercial packaging to protect such items as electrical goods makes an ideal drainage material. Break it up and use in the bottom of all containers when preparing for potting.

Pink and white impatiens look well with grey foliage plants, as seen here.

INDEX